Air and Weather

Developed at
Lawrence Hall of Science
University of California at Berkeley

Published and Distributed by **Delta Education**

ISBN 1-58356-833-6

542-2032

5 6 7 8 9 10 SPC 09 08 07 06 05

Table of Contents

What Is All around Us?

We can't see it, but it's all around.
It's in the sky.
It's in the treetops.
It's on the ground.
It's near and far, high and low.
What is it?

Air! We cannot see air, but we know it is there. What happens when you blow up a balloon? You fill it with air. You can see that air takes up space.

You also can feel air on your skin when the wind blows. Wind is moving air.

We can tell that air is there when we fly a kite. The wind pushes against the kite and keeps it in the sky.

We can tell that air is there when a parachute floats to the ground. Air pushes up against the parachute so it comes down slowly.

Even this boat shows us that air is all around. Propellers on the back of the boat push on the air. The boat moves forward.

So, what is all around us, everywhere we go? You know!

What's the Weather Today?

Lots of things happen in the air. The temperature can change from warm to cold. Clouds may form and rain may fall. The wind can start to blow. The condition of the air at a certain time is called weather.

How do you know what the weather will be today? One way to find out is to look outside. If the sky is dark and cloudy, you know it might rain.

If it is sunny, you know it won't rain—at least not right away.

Clouds are made of little drops of water. If there is a lot of water in a cloud, the cloud looks gray. The water drops may get bigger and bigger. They may fall as rain.

Or, if the air is cold enough, it snows instead.

Some days it looks as if clouds are sitting on the ground, instead of floating in the sky. The air feels wet, and you can't see very far. These clouds near the ground are called fog.

The weather you see when you look outside may change. A day may start out bright and sunny.

Later, clouds may form. Soon, the sky is filled with them.

If there is enough water in the clouds and the drops get big enough, it will rain. A storm can blow in and out in an afternoon. Or, a storm can stay around for days.

Weather is in the air.
And air is all around you.
You feel and see the weather,
every day, all the time.
So, go outside.
Enjoy the weather.
It may change tomorrow!

Understanding the Weather

Some people study the weather. They are called meteorologists. They use instruments to gather information about the weather. Meteorologists measure the temperature of the air. They watch clouds form. They measure wind speed and direction.

Weather balloons carry weather instruments high into the sky. The weather instruments gather information. This information helps meteorologists tell us what the weather will be.

Sometimes weather is dangerous. Meterologists can be helpful at these times. They can help us know when to get ready for a storm.

A tornado is a twirling, cloudy storm. A tornado's winds blow around and around very quickly.

A hurricane is a very big, strong, wet storm. Hurricanes form over warm ocean water.

Lightning can be dangerous.
It is important to learn safety rules
to be prepared for storms.

Seasons

In many areas, the seasons bring different kinds of weather.

Fall

Leaves change color
and drop from the trees.
Squirrels find food for the winter.
A cool wind blows.
We put on our sweatshirts
to play in the leaves of autumn.

Winter

Trees stand bare.
Few animals stir.
Snow starts to fall to the ground.
We bundle up
to keep ourselves warm
before we go sledding outdoors.

Spring

Leaves grow on trees.
Flowers bloom.
Birds are building their nests.
The air warms up,
and we go out to play
in the warm, soft breezes of spring.

Summer

The sun shines brightly
on a hot summer day.
There isn't a cloud in the sky.
The trees give us shade.
We can make lemonade.
Then we're off to the beach nearby.

The seasons can make everything look different. Which season do you see in each picture? How can you tell?

Glossary

Cloud - a group of very tiny water drops in the sky.

Measure - to find the amount of something, such as weight or size.

Meteorologist - a person who studies the weather.

Parachute - a piece of cloth that catches air to slow a person or object that is falling.

Propeller - blades that turn around a center point to push or blow air.

Storm - weather that has strong winds and can bring rain or snow.

Temperature - a description of how hot or cold something is.

Weather - the condition of the air at a given time.

Weather balloon - a balloon used to carry weather instruments into the sky.

Weather instrument - a tool that helps meteorologists measure weather.